SHALL WE GATHER AT THE RIVER

Und wenn der Mensch in seiner Qual verstummt,
Gab mir ein Gott zu sagen, was ich leide.

(Goethe)

SHALL

WE

GATHER

AT THE

RIVER

BY

James Wright

WESLEYAN UNIVERSITY PRESS

Middletown, Connecticut

For permission to reprint some of these poems, the author wishes to make due acknowledgement to the editors of the following magazines: *Chicago Review, Choice, Hudson Review, Minnesota Review, The Nation,* and *Stand;* also to Scott, Foresman and Company, publishers of *The Distinctive Voice* edited by William J. Martz.

"Confession to J. Edgar Hoover" was first printed in *Chelsea.*

The following poems originally appeared in *The New Yorker:* "Before a Cashier's Window in a Department Store," "For the Marsh's Birthday," "Poems to a Brown Cricket," and "Speak."

The following poems first appeared in *Poetry:* "The Life," "The Lights in the Hallway," "Listening to Mourners," "Old Age Compensation," and "Outside Fargo, North Dakota."

"I Am a Sioux Brave, He Said in Minneapolis," "In Memory of Leopardi," "Lifting Illegal Nets by Flashlight," and "Living by the Red River" had their initial publication in *The Sixties.*

Library of Congress Catalog Card Number : 68–27545

Manufactured in the United States of America

First printing September 1968; second printing November 1968

Jenny

CONTENTS

SHALL WE GATHER AT THE RIVER

Good evening, Charlie. Yes, I know. You rise,
Two lean gray spiders drifting through your eyes.
Poor Charlie, hobbling down the hill to find
The last bootlegger who might strike them blind,
Be dead. A child, I saw you hunch your spine,
Wrench your left elbow round, to hold in line
The left-hand hollow of your back, as though
The kidney prayed for mercy. Years ago.
The kidneys do not pray, the kidneys drip.
Urine stains at the liver; lip by lip,
Affectionate, the snub-nosed demons kiss
And sting us back to such a world as this.
Charlie, the moon drips slowly in the dark,
The mill smoke stains the snow, the gray whores walk,
The left-hand hollow fills up, like the tide
Drowning the moon, skillful with suicide.
Charlie, don't ask me. Charlie go away,
I feel my own spine hunching. If I pray,
I lose all meaning. I don't know my kind:
Sack me, or bury me among the blind.
What should I pray for? what can they forgive?
You died because you could not bear to live,
Pitched off the bridge in Brookside, God knows why.
Well, don't remind me. I'm afraid to die,
It hurts to die, although the lucky do.
Charlie, I don't know what to say to you
Except Good Evening, Greetings, and Good Night,
God Bless Us Every One. Your grave is white.
What are you doing here?

1.

I wonder how many old men last winter
Hungry and frightened by namelessness prowled
The Mississippi shore
Lashed blind by the wind, dreaming
Of suicide in the river.
The police remove their cadavers by daybreak
And turn them in somewhere.
Where?
How does the city keep lists of its fathers
Who have no names?
By Nicollet Island I gaze down at the dark water
So beautifully slow.
And I wish my brothers good luck
And a warm grave.

2.

The Chippewa young men
Stab one another shrieking
Jesus Christ.
Split-lipped homosexuals limp in terror of assault.
High school backfields search under benches
Near the Post Office. Their faces are the rich
Raw bacon without eyes.
The Walker Art Center crowd stare
At the Guthrie Theater.

3.

Tall Negro girls from Chicago
Listen to light songs.
They know when the supposed patron
Is a plainclothesman.

A cop's palm
Is a roach dangling down the scorched fangs
Of a light bulb.
The soul of a cop's eyes
Is an eternity of Sunday daybreak in the suburbs
Of Juárez, Mexico.

4.

The legless beggars are gone, carried away
By white birds.
The Artificial Limbs Exchange is gutted
And sown with lime.
The whalebone crutches and hand-me-down trusses
Huddle together dreaming in a desolation
Of dry groins.
I think of poor men astonished to waken
Exposed in broad daylight by the blade
Of a strange plough.

5.

All over the walls of comb cells
Automobiles perfumed and blindered
Consent with a mutter of high good humor
To take their two naps a day.
Without sound windows glide back
Into dusk.
The sockets of a thousand blind bee graves tier upon tier
Tower not quite toppling.
There are men in this city who labor dawn after dawn
To sell me my death.

6.

But I could not bear
To allow my poor brother my body to die
In Minneapolis.
The old man Walt Whitman our countryman
Is now in America our country
Dead.
But he was not buried in Minneapolis
At least.
And no more may I be
Please God.

7.

I want to be lifted up
By some great white bird unknown to the police,
And soar for a thousand miles and be carefully hidden
Modest and golden as one last corn grain,
Stored with the secrets of the wheat and the mysterious lives
Of the unnamed poor.

INSCRIPTION FOR THE TANK

My life was never so precious
To me as now.
I gape unbelieving at those two lines
Of my words, caught and frisked naked.

If they loomed secret and dim
On the wall of the drunk-tank,
Scraped there by a raw fingernail
In the trickling crusts of gray mold,

Surely the plainest thug who read them
Would cluck with the ancient pity.
Men have a right to thank God for their loneliness.
The walls are hysterical with their dank messages.

But the last hophead is gone
With the quick of his name
Bleeding away down a new wall
Blank as his nails.

I wish I had walked outside
To wade in the sea, drowsing and soothed;
I wish I had copied some words from Isaiah,
Kabir, Ansari, oh Whitman, oh anyone, anyone.

But I wrote down mine, and now
I must read them forever, even
When the wings in my shoulders cringe up
At the cold's fangs, as now.

Of all my lives, the one most secret to me,
Folded deep in a book never written,
Locked up in a dream of a still place,
I have blurted out.

I have heard weeping in secret
And quick nails broken.
Let the dead pray for their own dead.
What is their pity to me?

I still have some money
To eat with, alone
And frightened, knowing how soon
I will waken a poor man.

It snows freely and freely hardens
On the lawns of my hope, my secret
Hounded and flayed. I wonder
What words to beg money with.

Pardon me, sir, could you?
Which way is St. Paul?
I thirst.
I am a full-blooded Sioux Indian.

Soon I am sure to become so hungry
I will have to leap barefoot through gas-fire veils of shame,
I will have to stalk timid strangers
On the whorsehouse corners.

Oh moon, sow leaves on my hands,
On my seared face, oh I love you.
My throat is open, insane,
Tempting pneumonia.

But my life was never so precious
To me as now.
I will have to beg coins
After dark.

I will learn to scent the police,
And sit or go blind, stay mute, be taken for dead
For your sake, oh my secret,
My life.

1.

He is just plain drunk.
He knows no more than I do
What true waters to mourn for
Or what kind of words to sing
When he dies.

2.

The black caterpillar
Crawls out, what with one thing
And another, across
The wet road.
How lonely the dead must be.

The great cracked shadow of the Sierra Nevada
Hoods over the last road.

I came down here from the side of
A cold cairn where a girl named Rachel
Just made it inside California
And died of bad luck.

Here, across from the keno board,
An old woman
Has been beating a strange machine
In its face all day.

Dusk limps past in the street.
I step outside.
It's gone.
I finger a worthless agate
In my pocket.

Well, I still have a train ticket valid.
I can get out.
The faces of unimaginably beautiful blind men
Glide among mountains.
What pinnacles should they gaze upon
Except the moon?
Eight miles down in the secret canyons and ranges
Of six o'clock, the poor
Are mountainously blind and invisible.
Do they die?
Where are they buried?
They fill the sea now.
When you glide in, men cast shadows
You can trace from an airplane.
Their shoulders are huge with the barnacles
That God has cast down into the deep places.
The Sixth Day remained evening, deepening further down,
Further and further down, into night, a wounded black angel
Forgotten by Genesis.
If only the undulating of the shadows would pause.
The sea can stand anything.
I can't.

I can remember the evening.
I can remember the morning.
I am too young
To live in the sea alone without
Any company.
I can either move into the McCormick Theological Seminary
And get a night's sleep,
Or else get hauled back to Minneapolis.

Morgan the lonely,
Morgan the dead,
Has followed his only
Child into a vast
Desolation.
When I heard he was going
I tried to blossom
Into the boat beside him,
But I had no money.

When I went in to see him,
The nurse said no.
So I snuck in behind her.
And there they were.
They were there, for a moment.
Red Jacket, Robert Hayman,
H. Phelps Putnam,
And sweet Ted Roethke,
A canary and a bear.

They looked me over,
More or less alive.
They looked at me, more
Or less out of place.
They said, get out,
Morgan is dying.
They said, get out,
Leave him alone.

We have no kings
In this country,
They kept saying.

But we have one
Where the dead rise
On the other shore.
And they hear only
The cold owls throwing
Salt over
Their secret shoulders.

So I left Morgan,
And all of them alone.
And now I am so lonely
For the air l want to breathe.
Come breathe me, dark prince.
And Morgan lay there
Clean shaved like a baby
By the nurse who said no.
And so a couple
Of years ago,
The old poets died
Young.

And now the young,
Scarlet on their wings, fly away
Over the marshes.

There are no roads but the frost,
And the pumpkins look haggard.
The ants have gone down to the grave, crying
God spare them one green blade.
Failing the grass, they have abandoned the grass.
All creatures who have died today of old age
Have gone more than ten miles already.
All day I have slogged behind
And dreamed of them praying for one candle,
Only one.
Fair enough. Only, from where I stand,
I can see one last night nurse shining in one last window
In the Home for Senior Citizens.
The white uniform flickers, the town is gone.
What do I do now? I have one candle,
But what's the use?
If only they can catch up with twilight,
They'll be safe enough.
Their boats are moored there, among the cattails
And the night-herons' nests.
All they have to do now
Is to get one of those lazy birds awake long enough
To guide them across the river.
Herons fly low, too.
All it will take is one old man trawling one oar.
Anybody can follow a blue wing,
They don't need my candle.
But I do.

BEFORE A CASHIER'S WINDOW IN A DEPARTMENT STORE

1.

The beautiful cashier's white face has risen once more
Behind a young manager's shoulder.
They whisper together, and stare
Straight into my face.
I feel like grabbing a stray child
Or a skinny old woman
And driving into a cellar, crouching
Under a stone bridge, praying myself sick,
Till the troops pass.

2.

Why should he care? He goes.
I slump deeper.
In my frayed coat, I am pinned down
By debt. He nods,
Commending my flesh to the pity of the daws of God.

3.

Am I dead? And, if not, why not?
For she sails there, alone, looming in the
        heaven of the beautiful.
She knows
The bulldozers will scrape me up
After dark, behind
The officers' club.
Beneath her terrible blaze, my skeleton
Glitters out. I am the dark. I am the dark
Bone I was born to be.

4.

Tu Fu woke shuddering on a battlefield
Once, in the dead of night, and made out
The mangled women, sorting
The haggard slant-eyes.
The moon was up.

5.

I am hungry. In two more days
It will be spring. So this
Is what it feels like.

To speak in a flat voice
Is all that I can do.
I have gone every place
Asking for you.
Wondering where to turn
And how the search would end
And the last streetlight spin
Above me blind.

Then I returned rebuffed
And saw under the sun
The race not to the swift
Nor the battle won.
Liston dives in the tank,
Lord, in Lewiston, Maine,
And Ernie Doty's drunk
In hell again.

And Jenny, oh my Jenny
Whom I love, rhyme be damned,
Has broken her spare beauty
In a whorehouse old.
She left her new baby
In a bus-station can,
And sprightly danced away
Through Jacksontown.

Which is a place I know,
One where I got picked up
A few shrunk years ago
By a good cop.
Believe it, Lord, or not.

Don't ask me who he was.
I speak of flat defeat
In a flat voice.

I have gone forward with
Some, a few lonely some.
They have fallen to death.
I die with them.
Lord, I have loved Thy cursed,
The beauty of Thy house:
Come down. Come down. Why dost
Thou hide thy face?

Along the sprawled body of the derailed
    Great Northern freight car,
I strike a match slowly and lift it slowly.
No wind.

Beyond town, three heavy white horses
Wade all the way to their shoulders
In a silo shadow.

Suddenly the freight car lurches.
The door slams back, a man with a flashlight
Calls me good evening.
I nod as I write good evening, lonely
And sick for home.

Blood flows in me, but what does it have to do
With the rain that is falling?
In me, scarlet-jacketed armies march into the rain
Across dark fields. My blood lies still,
Indifferent to cannons on the ships of imperialists
Drifting offshore.
Sometimes I have to sleep
In dangerous places, on cliffs underground,
Walls that still hold the whole prints
Of ancient ferns.

In Fargo, North Dakota, a man
Warned me the river might rise
To flood stage again.
On the bridge, a girl hurries past me, alone,
Unhappy face.
Will she pause in wet grass somewhere?
Behind my eyes she stands tiptoe, yearning
        for confused sparrows
To fetch a bit of string and dried wheatbeard
To line her outstretched hand.
I open my eyes and gaze down
At the dark water.

A POEM WRITTEN UNDER AN ARCHWAY IN A DISCONTINUED
RAILROAD STATION, FARGO, NORTH DAKOTA

Outside the great clanging cathedrals of rust and smoke,
The locomotives browse on sidings.
They pause, exhausted by the silence of prairies.
Sometimes they leap and cry out, skitterish.
They fear dark little boys in Ohio,
Who know how to giggle without breathing,
Who sneak out of graveyards in summer twilights
And lay crossties across rails.
The rattle of coupling pins still echoes
In the smoke stains,
The Cincinnati of the dead.
Around the bend now, beyond the grain elevators,
The late afternoon limited wails
Savage with the horror and loneliness of a child, lost
And dragged by a glad cop through a Chicago terminal.
The noose tightens, the wail stops, and I am leaving.
Across the street, an arthritic man
Takes coins at the parking lot.
He smiles with the sinister grief
Of old age.

Today I am walking alone in a bare place,
And winter is here.
Two squirrels near a fence post
Are helping each other drag a branch
Toward a hiding place; it must be somewhere
Behind those ash trees.
They are still alive, they ought to save acorns
Against the cold.
Frail paws rifle the troughs between cornstalks
    when the moon
Is looking away.
The earth is hard now,
The soles of my shoes need repairs.
I have nothing to ask a blessing for,
Except these words.
I wish they were
Grass.

The man on the radio mourns
That another endless American winter
Daybreak is beginning to fall
On Idaho, on the mountains.

How many scrawny children
Lie dead and half-hidden among frozen ruts
In my body, along my dark roads.
Lean coyotes pass among clouds
On mountain trails, and smile,
And pass on in snow.

A girl stands in a doorway.
Her arms are bare to the elbows,
Her face gray, she stares coldly
At the daybreak.
When the howl goes up, her eyes
Flare white, like a mare's.

Crouched down by a roadside windbreak
At the edge of the prairie,
I flinch under the baleful jangling of wind
Through the telephone wires, a wilderness of voices
Blown for a thousand miles, for a hundred years.
They all have the same name, and the name is lost.
So: it is not me, it is not my love
Alone lost.
The grief that I hear is my life somewhere.
Now I am speaking with the voice
Of a scarecrow that stands up
And suddenly turns into a bird.
This field is the beginning of my native land,
This place of skull where I hear myself weeping.

Strange bird,
His song remains secret.
He worked too hard to read books.
He never heard how Sherwood Anderson
Got out of it, and fled to Chicago, furious to free himself
From his hatred of factories.
My father toiled fifty years
At Hazel-Atlas Glass,
Caught among girders that smash the kneecaps
Of dumb honyaks.
Did he shudder with hatred in the cold shadow of grease?
Maybe. But my brother and I do know
He came home as quiet as the evening.

He will be getting dark, soon,
And loom through new snow.
I know his ghost will drift home
To the Ohio River, and sit down, alone,
Whittling a root.
He will say nothing.
The waters flow past, older, younger
Than he is, or I am.

It can't be the passing of time that casts
That white shadow across the waters
Just offshore.
I shiver a little, with the evening.
I turn down the steep path to find
What's left of the river gold.
I whistle a dog lazily, and lazily
A bird whistles me.
Close by a big river, I am alive in my own country,
I am home again.
Yes: I lived here, and here, and my name,
That I carved young, with a girl's, is healed over, now,
And lies sleeping beneath the inward sky
Of a tree's skin, close to the quick.
It's best to keep still.
But:
There goes that bird that whistled me down here
To the river a moment ago.
Who is he? A little white barn owl from Hudson's Bay,
Flown out of his range here, and lost?
Oh, let him be home here, and, if he wants to,
He can be the body that casts
That white shadow across the waters
Just offshore.

Murdered, I went, risen,
Where the murderers are,
That black ditch
Of river.

And if I come back to my only country
With a white rose on my shoulder,
What is that to you?
It is the grave
In blossom.

It is the trillium of darkness,
It is hell, it is the beginning of winter,
It is a ghost town of Etruscans who have no names
Any more.

It is the old loneliness.
It is.
And it is
The last time.

1.

There they are now,
The wings,
And I heard them beginning to starve
Between two cold white shadows,
But I dreamed they would rise
Together,
My black Ohioan swan.

2.

Now one after another I let the black scales fall
From the beautiful black spine
Of this lonesome dragon that is born on the earth at last,
My black fire,
Ovoid of my darkness,
Machine-gunned and shattered hillsides of yellow trees
In the autumn of my blood where the apples
Purse their wild lips and smirk knowingly
That my love is dead.

3.

Here, carry his splintered bones
Slowly, slowly
Back into the
Tar and chemical strangled tomb,
The strange water, the
Ohio river, that is no tomb to
Rise from the dead
From.

In this field,
Where the small animals ran from a brush fire,
It is a voice
In burned weeds, saying
I love you.

Still, when I go there,
I find only two gray stones,
And, lying between them,
A dead bird the color of slate.
It lies askew in its wings,
Its throat bent back as if at the height
        of some joy too great
To bear to give.

And the lights are going out
In a farmhouse, evening
Stands, in a gray frock, silent, at the far side
Of a raccoon's grave.

The lights in the hallway
Have been out a long time.
I clasp her,
Terrified by the roundness of the earth
And its apples and the voluptuous rings
Of poplar trees, the secret Africas,
The children they give us.
She is slim enough.
Her knee feels like the face
Of a surprised lioness
Nursing the lost children
Of a gazelle by pure accident.
In that body I long for,
The Gabon poets gaze for hours
Between boughs toward heaven, their noble faces
Too secret to weep.
How do I know what color her hair is? I float among
Lonely animals, longing
For the red spider who is God.

1.

He is not the last one.
I wish he were. Do I?
My friends brought him into the kitchen
In a waste basket and
Took him out and
Set him down.
I stroked his long throat
On the floor. I was glad to hear him
Croaking with terror.

2.

The Nazis assigned
A dour man
To drive a truck every morning.
They called him "King of the Jews."
One evening, a dour man,
An Old Jew, sought out the King.
"You! Schmo! When you pick me up tomorrow,
Put me on top of the stack,
I've got asthma."

3.

He is not the last one. There is a darkening place
Among the cattails on the other side of the river.
The blue heron has gone there this evening,
Darkening into a reed that the fastidious fox
Never dreamed of.

My uncle, a craftsman of hammers and wood,
Is dead in Ohio.
And my mother cries she is angry.
Willy was buried with nothing except a jacket
Stitched on his shoulder bones.
It is nothing to mourn for.
It is the other world.
She does not know how the roan horses, there,
Dead for a century,
Plod slowly.
Maybe they believe Willy's brown coffin, tangled heavily
    in moss,
Is a horse trough drifted to shore
Along that river under the willows and grass.
Let my mother weep on, she needs to, she knows of cold winds.
The long box is empty.
The horses turn back toward the river.
Willy planes limber trees by the waters,
Fitting his boat together.
We may as well let him go.
Nothing is left of Willy on this side
But one cracked ball-peen hammer and one suit,
Including pants, his son inherited,
For a small fee, from Hesslop's funeral home;
And my mother,
Weeping with anger, afraid of winter
For her brothers' sake:
Willy, and John, whose life and art, if any,
I never knew.

1.

The anguish of a naked body is more terrible
To bear than God.
And the rain goes on falling.

2.

When I stand up to cry out,
She laughs.
On the window sill, I lean
My bare elbows.
One blue wing, torn whole out of heaven,
Soaks in the black rain.

3.

Blind, mouth sealed, a face blazes
On my pillow of cold ashes.

4.

No!
I kneel down, naked, and ask forgiveness.
A cold drizzle blows into the room,
And my shoulders flinch to the bone.
You have nothing to do with us.
Sleep on.

I have gone past all those times when the poets
Were beautiful as only
The rich can be. The cold bangles
Of the moon grazed one of my shoulders,
And so to this day,
And beyond, I carry
The sliver of a white city, the barb of a jewel
In my left clavicle that hunches.
Tonight I sling
A scrambling sack of oblivions and lame prayers
On my right good arm. The Ohio River
Has flown by me twice, the dark jubilating
Isaiah of mill and smoke marrow. Blind son
Of a meadow of huge horses, lover of drowned islands
Above Steubenville, blind father
Of my halt gray wing:
Now I limp on, knowing
The moon strides behind me, swinging
The scimitar of the divinity that struck down
The hunchback in agony
When he saw her, naked, carrying away his last sheep
Through the Asian rocks.

1.

Tonight I watch my father's hair,
As he sits dreaming near his stove.
Knowing my feather of despair,
He sent me an owl's plume for love,
Lest I not know, so I've come home.
Tonight Ohio, where I once
Hounded and cursed my loneliness,
Shows me my father, who broke stones,
Wrestled and mastered great machines,
And rests, shadowing his lovely face.

2.

Nobly his hands fold together in his repose.
He is proud of me, believing
I have done strong things among men and become a man
Of place among men of place in the large cities.
I will not waken him.
I have come home alone, without wife or child
To delight him. Awake, solitary and welcome,
I too sit near his stove, the lines
Of an ugly age scarring my face, and my hands
Twitch nervously about.

As a father to his son, as a friend to
his friend, Be pleased to show mercy, O God.

I was alone once, waiting
For you, what you might be.
I heard your grass birds, fluting
Down a long road, to me.
Wholly for you, for you,
I was lonely, lonely.

For how was I to know
Your voice, or understand
The Irish cockatoo?
Never on sea or land
Had I heard a voice that was
Greener than grass.

Oh the voice lovelier was
Than a crow's dreaming face,
His secret face, that smiles
Alive in a dead place.
Oh I was lonely, lonely:
What were the not to me?

The not were nothing then.
Now, let the not become
Nothing, and so remain,
Till the bright grass birds come
Home to the singing tree.
Then, let them be.

/47

Let them be living, then,
They have been dead so long.
Love, I am sick of pain
And sick with my longing,
My Irish cockatoo,
To listen to you,

Now you are all alive
And not a dream at all;
Now there are more than five
Voices I listen to
Call, call, call, call, call, call:
My Irish cockatoo.

The carp are secrets
Of the creation: I do not
Know if they are lonely.
The poachers drift with an almost frightening
Care under the bridge.
Water is a luminous
Mirror of swallows' nests. The stars
Have gone down.
What does my anguish
Matter? Something
The color
Of a puma has plunged through this net, and is gone.
This is the firmest
Net I ever saw, and yet something
Is gone lonely
Into the headwaters of the Minnesota.

Hiding in the church of an abandoned stone,
A Negro soldier
Is flipping the pages of the Articles of War,
That he can't read.

Our father,
Last evening I devoured the wing
Of a cloud.
And, in the city, I sneaked down
To pray with a sick tree.

I labor to die, father,
I ride the great stones,
I hide under stars and maples,
And yet I cannot find my own face.
In the mountains of blast furnaces,
The trees turn their backs on me.

Father, the dark moths
Crouch at the sills of the earth, waiting.

And I am afraid of my own prayers.
Father, forgive me.
I did not know what I was doing.

You strolled in the open, leisurely and alone,
Daydreaming of a beautiful human body
That had undressed quietly and slipped into the river
And become the river:
The proud body of an animal that would transform
The snaggled gears and the pulleys
Into a plant that grows under water.
You went searching gently for the father of your own agony,
The camellia of your death,
The voice that would call out to you clearly and name the fires
Of your hidden equator.

Solitary,
Patient for the last voices of the dusk to die down, and the dusk
To die down, listener waiting for courteous rivers
To rise and be known,
You kept a dark counsel.
It is not seemly a man should rend open by day
The huge roots of his blood trees.
A man ought to hide sometimes on the banks
Of the sky,
And some human beings
Have need of lingering back in the fastidious half-light
Even at dawn.

Under the enormous pier-shadow,
Hobie Johnson drowned in a suckhole.
I cannot even remember
His obliterated face.
Outside my window, now, Minneapolis
Drowns, dark.
It is dark.
I have no life.

What is left of all of it?
Blind hoboes sell American flags
And bad poems of patriotism
On Saturday evenings forever in the rain,
Between the cathouses and the slag heaps
And the river, down home.
Oh Jesus Christ, the Czechoslovakians
Are drunk again, clambering
Down the sand-pitted walls
Of the grave.

IN RESPONSE TO A RUMOR THAT THE OLDEST WHOREHOUSE IN WHEELING, WEST VIRGINIA, HAS BEEN CONDEMNED

I will grieve alone,
As I strolled alone, years ago, down along
The Ohio shore.
I hid in the hobo jungle weeds
Upstream from the sewer main,
Pondering, gazing.

I saw, down river,
At Twenty-third and Water Streets
By the vinegar works,
The doors open in early evening.
Swinging their purses, the women
Poured down the long street to the river
And into the river.

I do not know how it was
They could drown every evening.
What time near dawn did they climb up the other shore,
Drying their wings?

For the river at Wheeling, West Virginia
Has only two shores:
The one in hell, the other
In Bridgeport, Ohio.

And nobody would commit suicide, only
To find beyond death
Bridgeport, Ohio.

1.

I woke,
Just about daybreak, and fell back
In a drowse.
A clean leaf from one of the new cedars
Has blown in through the open window.
How long ago a huge shadow of wings pondering and hovering
　　leaned down
To comfort my face.
I don't care who loved me.
Somebody did, so I let myself alone.
I will stand watch for you, now.
I lay here awake a long time before I looked up
And found you sunning yourself asleep
In the Secret Life of Jakob Boehme
Left open on the desk.

2.

Our friends gave us their love
And this room to sleep in.
Outside now, not a sound.
Instead of rousing us out for breakfast,
Our friends love us and grant us our loneliness.
We shall waken again
When the courteous face of the old horse David
Appears at our window,
To snuffle and cough gently.
He, too, believes we may long for
One more dream of slow canters across the prairie
Before we come home to our strange bodies
And rise from the dead.

3.

As for me, I have been listening,
For an hour or so, now, to the scampering ghosts
Of Sioux ponies, down the long road
Toward South Dakota.
They just brought me home, leaning forward, by both hands
    clinging
To the joists of the magnificent dappled feathers
Under their wings.

4.

As for you, I won't press you to tell me
Where you have gone.
I know. I know how you love to edge down
The long trails of canyons.
At the bottom, along willow shores, you stand, waiting for twilight,
In the silence of deep grass.
You are safe there, guarded, for you know how the dark faces
Of the cliffs forbid easy plundering
Of their beautiful pueblos:
White cities concealed delicately in their chasms
As the new eggs of the mourning dove
In her ground nest,
That only the spirit hunters
Of the snow can find.

5.

Brown cricket, you are my friend's name.
I will send back my shadow for your sake, to stand guard
On the solitude of the mourning dove's young.
Here, I will stand by you, shadowless,
At the small golden door of your body till you wake
In a book that is shining.

It is all right. All they do
Is go in by dividing
One rib from another. I wouldn't
Lie to you. It hurts
Like nothing I know. All they do
Is burn their way in with a wire.
It forks in and out a little like the tongue
Of that frightened garter snake we caught
At Cloverfield, you and me, Jenny
So long ago.

I would lie to you
If I could.
But the only way I can get you to come up
Out of the suckhole, the south face
Of the Powhatan pit, is to tell you
What you know:

You come up after dark, you poise alone
With me on the shore.
I lead you back to this world.

Three lady doctors in Wheeling open
Their offices at night.
I don't have to call them, they are always there.
But they only have to put the knife once
Under your breast.
Then they hang their contraption.
And you bear it.

/57

It's awkward a while. Still, it lets you
Walk about on tiptoe if you don't
Jiggle the needle.
It might stab your heart, you see.
The blade hangs in your lung and the tube
Keeps it draining.
That way they only have to stab you
Once. Oh Jenny,
I wish to God I had made this world, this scurvy
And disastrous place. I
Didn't, I can't bear it
Either, I don't blame you, sleeping down there
Face down in the unbelievable silk of spring,
Muse of black sand,
Alone.

I don't blame you, I know
The place where you lie.
I admit everything. But look at me.
How can I live without you?
Come up to me, love,
Out of the river, or I will
Come down to you.

Distinguished contemporary poetry in cloth and paperback editions

ALAN ANSEN: *Disorderly Houses* (1961)

JOHN ASHBERY: *The Tennis Court Oath* (1962)

ROBERT BAGG: *Madonna of the Cello* (1961)

MICHAEL BENEDIKT: *The Body* (1968)

ROBERT BLY: *Silence in the Snowy Fields* (1962)

TURNER CASSITY: *Watchboy, What of the Night?* (1966)

TRAM COMBS: *saint thomas. poems.* (1965)

DONALD DAVIE: *Events and Wisdoms* (1965); *New and Selected Poems* (1961)

JAMES DICKEY: *Buckdancer's Choice* (1965) [National Book Award in Poetry, 1966]; *Drowning With Others* (1962); *Helmets* (1964)

DAVID FERRY: *On the Way to the Island* (1960)

ROBERT FRANCIS: *The Orb Weaver* (1960)

JOHN HAINES: *Winter News* (1966)

EDWIN HONIG: *Spring Journal: Poems* (1968)

RICHARD HOWARD: *The Damages* (1967); *Quantities* (1962)

BARBARA HOWES: *Light and Dark* (1959)

DAVID IGNATOW: *Figures of the Human* (1964); *Rescue the Dead* (1968); *Say Pardon* (1961)

DONALD JUSTICE: *Night Light* (1967); *The Summer Anniversaries* (1960) [A Lamont Poetry Selection]

CHESTER KALLMAN: *Absent and Present* (1963)

PHILIP LEVINE: *Not This Pig* (1968)

LOU LIPSITZ: *Cold Water* (1967)

JOSEPHINE MILES: *Kinds of Affection* (1967)

VASSAR MILLER: *My Bones Being Wiser* (1963); *Onions and Roses* (1968); *Wage War on Silence* (1960)

W. R. MOSES: *Identities* (1965)

DONALD PETERSEN: *The Spectral Boy* (1964)

MARGE PIERCY: *Breaking Camp* (1968)

HYAM PLUTZIK: *Apples from Shinar* (1959)

VERN RUTSALA: *The Window* (1964)

HARVEY SHAPIRO: *Battle Report* (1966)

JON SILKIN: *Poems New and Selected* (1966)

LOUIS SIMPSON: *At the End of the Open Road* (1963) [Pulitzer Prize in Poetry, 1964]; *A Dream of Governors* (1959)

JAMES WRIGHT: *The Branch Will Not Break* (1963); *Saint Judas* (1959); *Shall We Gather at the River* (1968)